caught in
the light

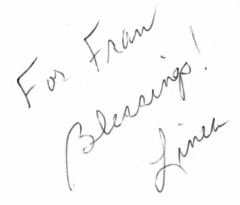

For Fran
Blessings!
Linda

caught in the light

Linea Reimer Geiser

ISBN: 1-4033-8615-3 (e-book)
ISBN: 1-4033-8616-1 (Paperback)

This book is printed on acid free paper.

Cover and Graphic Design by Dee Birkey

1stBooks - rev. 12/28/02

a small spill of words

for my family

Table of Contents

the past is
    dripping through

Sing for the Claw Foot Tub of Childhood

When summer sticks to me—
straw from the threshing machine
imbedded in my flaxen braids
gumbo (rich enough to push Grandmother's
glorious hollyhocks to the sky)
thick between my toes—
pour a high clear stream
from your ancient taps
wash away today
douse me with tomorrow

But water slips like dreams
the past is dripping through

O claw foot tub of childhood
everything intermingles
everything collides

Linea Reimer Geiser

For Saturday Night

Beat the hooked rugs, shine linoleum patterns
order chicken from Agnes, a list from the store
while the dough rises higher and promises, promises
crusty brown bread and buns by the score

Raspberry jam with the sweet tang of summer
creamery butter that spreads golden sun
chunks of sharp cheddar and ice-green dill pickles
a jar of bright cherries—the Blue Ribbon one

Come little dumplings and sit round our table
my best cloth is laid with small pleasures that last
Father will lead as we praise the Creator
a chanted refrain echoed down through our past

Little Mennonite Girl in the City

Awestruck I watch the parade
high heels tap tap
through Saturday night heat
click down the sidewalk
sashay down the city street
short skirts sliding against
slim supple hips
pouty lips, dark red party lips
on their way to pleasure

Ukranian, Irish, Italian, French
neighbor girls I don't know
dressed up in their dancing shoes
foreign, full of mystery to me
not like my sisters sitting circumspectly
not like my modest mother
fantasy girls looking just like
I want to look
when I reach seventeen

Linea Reimer Geiser

Spring Revival

Does one have to be sixteen to remember
when the air shouts
of melting snow piles, dares
to bare dandelion worlds, the misplaced taste
of green? In Manitoba prairie towns
when Alberta chinooks swaggered through
on any surprised spring afternoon
who could keep from being swept
into the clash of hot and cold
It was for more than summer that we yearned
as we stripped of caps and scarves, jackets
and mittens, desperate for any light touch
against our lonely skin

Spring, that season of danger
when all our repressions strained
at their winter seams
No wonder it was in spring that the revival
preachers blew in
collapsing our feathery dreams

Stumbling through Lent

"ashes, ashes
we all fall down"

what do I know of ashes
dancing ring-around-a-rosy
and I am Rosy among my
flaxen-braided friends

ashes come from warmth
wood and coal
fed into the silver
belly of our ancient furnace
its great sausage pipes
blasting heat into
all but the north-most rooms
my father scoops ashes
light as fluff

shovels of
innocent ashes good
for the summer garden

I know ashes
dropping softly
tapped by my father's nicotine-stained finger
into his empty coffee cup

cups of ashes, death by ashes
but not yet and I don't know the future

Linea Reimer Geiser

ashes
the sky will bloom with ashes
for now I hear faintly
a ranting in my ears
a word I do not know
"sieg heil" in the language
we reserve for church
but this is no sound
that's holy

later when the sirens of peace
wail the end of war and I am older
I hear of a fiery furnace
and screaming children

ashes floating in the wind
still a world of ashes

"ashes, ashes
we all fall down"

First Love

In the seclusion of Grandfather's lilacs
still green beneath the gravel dust
of Saturday night
small town
Main Street cruisers

We kissed—
innocents
still green beneath the swell
of our newly blooming bodies
two Main Street kids—
our Saturday night
cruising fingertips
uncurling a silky scent

Linea Reimer Geiser

In Celebration of Legs

I love my legs
my mother's legs
part of my inheritance
along with her china cabinet
and cast iron skillet

an adornment, an eye catcher
I examine their reflection in the mirror
starting from the bottom
ankles slender enough to peek beneath
Victorian petticoats
calves that survived trekking in Nepal, the ups and
downs of tending to a grandchild, the deep knee
bends of flower gardening
and thighs, thighs for a lover's eye

I celebrate long legs
long enough to sprint for pure pleasure
long enough to win races against old age
legs meant for stretching, stretching
like a ballerina straining in her sleep
for height

I honor these hardy legs that propel me
through this world
and will step me high
into the next

Love Grammar

I touch you
tenderly
You are a noun
a person, place, or thing
a Proper noun

We act
together
Slowly, deliberately
we verb

Wife

There she lies
propped up on sun-browned arms
her breasts dangling
like peaches waiting
to be plucked and sucked
for summer sweetness

She, too, is ancient goddess
Aztec Mother Earth
deftly extracting
the male heart
demanding the dripping
ventricles and chambers
that adore her

Like Coatlicue
carved in cataclysmic stone
passive beneath cathedral floors
she bides her time

First Goodbyes

I leave behind
only the empty pod
for the baby ghosts
pink and yellow
sleepered feet
scampering through
the morning of our marriage
are hiding in my marrow

Flower Cycles

After the rains
"the grandmothers" perk up
nod silky petals in their flower beds
catch comments now and then
from tight-rope perching doves
above and cardinals

I   Mother
Lythrum holds up its
purple spikes like an Indian
goddess with endless arms promising
everything

My mother grew lythrum
right next to our back door
When you picked green beans
in the garden patch
you could look out and see
bees on their morning detail checking
its thousands of tiny busy blooms

She cut arm loads
carried circles of purple
to the table we gathered
round for meals
I grow lythrum for her

14

II   Grossmama

This year the red geraniums
hurt your eyes
Mr. Peters' Professional Bloom Booster
shoots nitrogen up their stems
until they pump intensity
into the green heart of summer

Grossmama, short and round like all my father's kin
spruced up Main Street with window boxes
sprouting on every window of her house
and grew geraniums inside and out
so the whole town believed
like her troop of grandchildren
in her cheerful smile
She was jolly and loved
homefries and farmer sausage
roasted in its juices and
a multitude of pies and died
before the depression ended or
I slid into the doctor's red hands

My geraniums are for her
My hands smell like her hands
plunged into pungency

III   Step-Grandmother

Willowy, tall and willowy,
unusual in our tribe, but
dour—maybe
because her religion
dressed her in black
Step-mother to my mother,
the cosmos blooms for you
You grew it in rich black soil
till your doll-sized house marooned
itself in waves of color
pink, magenta, white, pleasing
your eyes and mine

Green stems hold up
summer petals, speak
for grandmothers
Waving in the breeze
"the grandmothers" perk up
after the rain

Cooking a Poem

My sap bubbles up
boils over
thick and rich
I scoop off the foam
before it's lost forever
and ladle it
into a poem
where it can cool
into sweetness
with a bite

like my Hungarian
Aunt Katherine
with the little moustache
above her upper lip
long dead
her belly laugh
as delicious
as metaphors

Linea Reimer Geiser

Winter Menu

I eat words when they
come to me
just like Jeremiah
suggests
My favorite today
for breakfast—"announced
by all the trumpets of the sky
arrives the snow"

I bet Jeremiah wished he had
been given those words
by raging Yahweh
instead of doom

but Emerson dished them up instead
What was his day like
Did he sit by the window
or trudge beside a pond
glorying in white
while I just opened up
the kitchen blinds and did a
quick red heart dance along
with cardinals feasting
on seeds and blue jays
raucous with hallelujahs

Tomorrow I will spread other words
on my morning toast

Change of Temperature

monochromatic day—gray
sky, street, old snow—black
rooftops, trees, lampposts
white flakes
floating

inside
among a smattering of books, rich
in warm worlds
time tipping I
dip and swoop, pick
continents, savor centuries
waiting
for an ancestor or two, ready
to join me in a cup of tea

suddenly Mother
no longer otherside
buried, cold
here, sweet and present
smiling

August Garden

Trimming thyme
baskets full of snipped herbs
scenting late summer

Oh could I heap time this way
wheelbarrows of it
hours fragrant with laughter
the taste of sunny mornings
early evenings steeped
in afterglow

Could I pile carts high with wonder
Len's sweet first kiss
his tender arms
holding me through
the decades

Could I plant years
the best days
a harvest of
anniversaries

reaching for
Grandmother Air

Creation Myth

Unfold
cries Father Universe
and like
a kaleidoscope
shards quiver, swirl, collide
retreat, expand
curl up and out
reaching
for Grandmother Air

Soon daffodils
of the mind
spiral yellow and green
singing

Linea Reimer Geiser

Afternoon in Eden

I lived a million years ago
when earth was young and wild
when sun shone white
and wind blew bright
and sea around me lapped this child
its powdery shore my toy

I dug my toes
I buried my hands
I reveled in shifting, shimmering sands
and sea rolled over in clean green joy

Spring Green

The first green of spring is
yellow, ask any child or
poet, creating the world
with sixty-four crayolas or
bright penned words

Just watch for willows among the
snow banks of the prairies
in early March, along the
river bends of your world

A hint of captured sun, not the bold statement
of the laburnums of Wales
gracing arbors
where you disappear under their
dazzling canopy

Think wisps of leaves
like line drawings, slender
billowing, draped against the sky
and delicious as shreds of lemon drops
lingering under your tongue

Linea Reimer Geiser

In this Place

In this place
a bird cries
a child calls
a warm wind washes the day
fills up surrounding space

Anchoring the morning
strong against the season's push
a blaze of forsythia
yellow as the sun
shouts praise

Sky Lights

I

Daffodils freeze dried
by April cold
still fill the night
with feathery moons

II

Midnight sky
slight breath against
my wind chimes
the night a crystal bowl
delicate as rain

III

Like the Son of God astride
his silver horse
shreds of heaven gleam, stream
across the dark canals of night
soak new grass in comet light
so even the raw trees
take on eternity

Linea Reimer Geiser

Chagall Windows

Oh
to take Mediterranean waves
on a morning in June
the shocking depth of Mexican skies
and Mother Mary's eyes
intent on love

Chagall
where did you
hear the call
to intensify the world
to blue

not the blue-black hole
of hell and Holocaust
sucking up breath and life
but the jewel of heaven
caught in the light

Summer Blue

Lake and sky shimmer blue
Skipping pebbles, the delicate dip
of dragonflies
barely break their surface

Blue sustains flight
across summer
But blue fools you

It lures you unless
you skim, it
drowns you in water, in air

Yet diving
is my necessity
to plunge into blue
my prayer

Linea Reimer Geiser

Heart Transplant

Wreathed in smiles
I plunge into the day
curl my hands in rich black soil
and laugh at the pillows of dirt
cushioning the tiny roots in my care

I will be gentle as a mist of rain
settle each plant into its Eden
bathe its tendrils with love and hormones
name it beautiful, graced with creation
mystery and gladly stain my knees
risk poison ivy and
roil my spine for the sake of
conspiring with God to tend
my flower bed

Yellow Leaves

I wade swish swish
through yellow waves
of maple leaves
shout glory glory to the glowing trees
catch drops of sun to drape
along my harvest table
say thank you thank you
to the autumn breeze

Deception

Ah, Autumn
You deceptive lover
You woo me with warm, windy fingers
As I reach for your ripeness
with practiced touch
you slip
cold winter's knife
between my ribs

North Wind

Countless sentinels
sensing speed and direction
fall grasses comb the surrounding sky
prepare survival tactics

Before your airy chariot
before your icy wheels
each blade submits to your tyranny
like shivering pale untouchables
each blade in your path salaams

Linea Reimer Geiser

Dressed for Waltzing

Just this moment
out my sparkling window
the trees are wearing clouds
their bare white bones
are dressed once more for waltzing
the festive winter ball
But clouds move on
and Cinderella trees
stand stripped, ungainly tall

Dream Journey

Praise the Lord of cumulus clouds
shifting the stars

Sing "Joy" to the midnight angel
the night-blooming poppies

Skip to the river and
collect small stones
with gentle hands lift them
before the sun rises
sift them sift them
into your cup of memory—
that dream catcher with sky trim

Then salute the alabaster horses
of morning galloping
galloping and ride
them home

Linea Reimer Geiser

Winter Canticle

I

white stars covering fields
turning tiny tots
winter wild

II

three jays commandeer
the bright blue sky claiming
the arctic air

sparrows fluffed for cold
a dozen feather puffs
warm my winter bush

barren branches
bloom red with Christmas
cardinals in snow

black sunflower hulls
dropped by juncos form crumbs
on snowy linen

caught by cold moonlight
pines glittering with snow
bewitch a blinking owl

III

when sun is a red surprise
lighting snow horizons
when each house shoots up ghost sentries
straight smoke plumes guarding still skies
when crunching footsteps mark but lightly
our gleaming passage

for all mornings nourished by severity
suckled on winter
thank you

IV

frozen Dutch canals
windswept Russian steppes
Canadian prairie blizzards
ghosts lodged in our family tree
drop into my morning

the cold of my ancestors calls me
I pull on my outer garments
drift outdoors
through diamonds glistening
in the sun
I dream of heaven—
long sweeps of sky
and white that blinds the eye
to everything but beauty

Geology

My collection of stones
includes granite from Mount Sinai
alabaster from Cairo
limestone from the Parthenon
plus beauties picked up along river beds
and the mountain paths of my life

I don't label them
I'm not a scientist
nobody except me
cares where I found them
and even I don't care carefully
but I keep them
in a cup of dreams
on my windowsill

Some stones I have only seen
locked behind glass
in museums
those I hoard in my memory
a rock from the moon
a meteor from Mars

Mozart Morning

When song
sings me over the mountain
I strain
for the faint ding of Eden
Let me catch
that lonely lovely giant bell
and tumble backwards
through eternity tolling

yellow dress

Yellow Dress

It's important to have older sisters
if you want to learn family history
mother stories about
me in her worn-out womb

Did you know my beautiful proud mother
bought a yellow dress
with big round buttons
like yellow moons adorning her
slender neck
saved pennies, one by one
sending my sisters to faraway
ma and pa stores once a week
for bargain hamburger
served eggs and bread and milk in between but
not enough so my sister
going on seven got rickets
and still saddens when she looks
in a full length mirror

My mother bought a yellow dress
to hide her thickened waist
pulled herself tall and prepared for
her sixth daughter long after she had
given her childbearing clothes to others
trying to give birth during the depression

45

Linea Reimer Geiser

I wish I could have seen her
soft brown hair caught in a bun
patrician nose inherited from some
foreign blood hidden in the family line

My mother, elegant and poor
in her yellow dress with yellow buttons
trailed by daughters
concealing me high under her ribs

Beginner

I am only
one small butterfly
known by a
postage-stamp square of sky
but I saddle the breeze

I'm bold, I'm brilliant
with wings unfurled
like miniature lariats
circling air
I rope in my world

Linea Reimer Geiser

Family System

Somewhere between layers of silk and satin and fur
the solid oak floors
shoved in with our high button shoes
witnessed solely by the tick of the painted clock
Great Grandfather carried from the Ukraine
we have misplaced a roaring psychosis

Earlier did the cells breed wildly or slow
on the wind swept steppes
in the authority of generations of father czars

How could even such dis-ease
withstand the purging
of old ways on the perilous sea sail
and first pioneer survival days

There, there
jumping between the beloved children
springs the danger
even while the round grandmother
rocks and croons her ancient songs

In the laughter, the indolent eyes
the jealous interplay, the confusion of daily life
grows the specter
until it bursts through all facades
faces us naked and ugly
demands its schizophrenic victim
a scapegoat to be secreted away
in the crazy house of our making

Writing Down the Bones

my sister
almost seventy
is writing down the bones
of our family

skeletons of
uncle william tricking his father
oppressing his submissive sister
uncle gerhard (by marriage) accused of stealing
the family farm

aunt sarah
vertebrae aligned
straight in the parlor rocker, singing
psalms to hallow
the family feuds

while little girls
my sisters, played
in the draughty hallways
climbed the old oak stairs
heard tales
told no one
until now

Linea Reimer Geiser

Klaas Reimer 1770-1837

I'm just starting to learn about
my great-great-great grandfather
never cared much to know his story before
I guess I had to be at least sixty and thinking
I'll soon (figuratively speaking) be spending eternity
with the ancestors so
we might as well get acquainted

His life is easy to trace
notorious for splintering a denomination
in 19th century Russia
not my favorite activity to promote
in this new millennium
at a time when some of his descendants
are trying desperately or at least judiciously
or something
to splice some earlier theological cracks

I grew up in his denomination, the "little congregation" that
moved en masse
from the steps of the Ukraine to
North America to keep the rigid faith intact

Maybe I laid too much on his shoulders
maybe he wasn't as strict, stern, pious
as I thought my preachers
asked me to be during my teens

I wondered about his wives—Maria, and later Helena
living with Klaas Reimer, founder of a flock devoted
to simplicity, narrow boundaries

Today I discovered the artist child tucked
inside his tall frame
Somewhere he found time to be a carver not only
of people but of wood—patiently working oak and ash
adding a curve or curlicue
to a chest, a pencil box, a cane
some lines flowing out and free

Linea Reimer Geiser

Elizabeth Dueck Toews
for my mother's mother

I can't get over her short life's work—
a litter of children—she drops one
each year until there are nine
to yearn for the warmth of her arms
the heavy belly that ferried
them into this world

A brand-new baby roots and snuffles
for her milky breast while the others cry
into their pillows in the cold upstairs
for Mama
falling into the sleep of the ages, rest at last
but such a cleaving, a leaving before
she has finished weaving
her family

She must have been beautiful
her children, now all dead
were beautiful
her grandchildren, great grandchildren
and great, yes, great grand grand
children who follow her
are strong and beautiful
woven of her cloth

Funeral Photo

for my father's mother

Outside her geranium window
Grandmother lies in state
while circles of drooping grandchildren
dot the lawns like flowers

Outside her sturdy house
beside the welcome porch
just yesterday the haunt
of sons and daughters courting
in its hide-and-seek vines
stands a sober remnant
ten living offspring wearing the family nose
surrounding their stricken father
lining up in sequence
as regular as Manitoba winters
to honor the matriarch
who gave them life
who descended
like dancing rain
across the prairie bush
out of the hinterland
peasant feet tapping

Linea Reimer Geiser

At Anna's Wake

She was so cold
not even eiderdown wrapped round her chin
could still her dread
that's why she wrung her hands so much
with nothing of her own to hold

Brief northern summers, green and clear
she waited for her Kansas beau to come for her
but since our mother's death she clung to Henry
store-keeper brother, self-crowned czar

She cooked his meals
green onions and a special flour in his bread
She sold his sun-paled wares, squeezed him profit
with each moldy orange she slipped into your sack

I could not make her take her medicine
although she feared the sudden jerky deaths
that seized her body as she scurried
through these dreary halls
I pled to have her live with me
and shed her squalor and her charge

Smell of garlic, smoke of burning bread
urine-tainted sheets, you soaked into her soul

This town, this house, this brother
Obsessed, she shattered in her stale cocoon
and on her only day of earthly honor
her tribute is my single wreath of flowers

Summer Savory

In July, Aunt Margaret
picked McKensie beans
quarts and quarts of them to last the winter
beans green and fuzzy
hiding in the leaves
dusted with early morning dew

I always knew where to find her
my eyes still brushed with dreams
I flung open the screen door of the big
white farmhouse
ran through the lattice garden arch

There, bent over
between the raspberry bushes
and the blooming hollyhocks
her ample body
flowery house dress clinging
to damp back and breasts
beans plopping into the blue enamel bowl

How was I so lucky
spending summer holidays with
this woman who was Earth Mother
full of family stories, rolling laughter
eyes squeezed tight with laughter
green bean soup for lunch
green beans scented with summer savory

Linea Reimer Geiser

The Taste of Love
for my mother and father

Brows furrowed in concentration
he plows his worn tires
across the dark landscape
through tiny towns
of bankrupt farmers
grafted unwillingly
onto the dole
but just until
the drought ends
then they'll buy
his green John Deeres again

He plucks determination
from the endless telephone poles
planted along each straight
mile of dust-blown prairie
catches summer in familiar night
sounds cheering him on, on, home
after five days on the dreary road

He sees the kitchen scene—
on the old oak table
her magenta cosmos blooming in a mason jar
survivors even of August sun
the ancient coffee pot brimming
on the back burner
at least there is still coffee

Another Friday night homecoming
and when he opens the door
she stands at the stove browning
the paper-thin slices of potatoes
fertilized with tears when
nothing else would grow

and for him, just for him
(there are not enough for the children)
two eggs cracked into the pan

Linea Reimer Geiser

My Father, the Salesman

my father, the salesman
bought one hundred dresses
his first dresses
the beginning of life
caressed each one
like a lover
rounded their curves
dreamt fierce dreams of
draping soft women
with wool and raw silk and
crepe de chine glory

built a round moon room
a window with circles
fitted the dresses in niches
lined them up on stiff hangers
his future
bright glowing
rich browns and dark navies
white collars and cuffs
prim, flowered
demurely for customers
pious

purred
come
to my moon room
buy beauty forbidden and
glamour
a dress for your husband
to take you to bed after
stripping you naked

58

close the lid of your endless
sewing and stitching
your life in neat patches
quilts of small boredoms

buy my wares
i, casanova
come to your village
straight from the city
selling you dreams

Expectations

When they swooped
back into my life
from that outer world that
my parents feared
my older sisters
came bearing gifts
like the magi

Queenly in
robes of extravagant love
they offered me

a song from the sea
a piece of sun from far away lands
a tiny madonna amulet
to grace my childhood neck

they brought a hint of romance
and golden possibilities
of a world beyond our village
and its insular dreams

What they asked of me
the youngest
was to shine like a star

Sister

First one
forced to give up the warm nest
of our mother
that floating heaven
of our earliest dreams
Out of deep safety
into a less inviting dark
you slid
anxious to please
a demanding audience
that asked too much
of your tiny willing heart
until you grew inch by bloody inch
from heel to curly head
a shiny core of steel
to hold you up
and anchor your quivering step

Does steel give enough
can you bend into fetal position
so in your sleep again
comes the curl of comfort
we call home sweet home

Linea Reimer Geiser

Hunter

In her other life
my sister, Mrs. D
shared her recipes in the
town cook book
for moose stew
venison steak—
her husband
then a wild hunter
long since dead

Now she is
Elizabeth
herself the hunter
tracking ancestral
trails
quietly stalking
her stories
cooking them into
poems and novels
their dark rich broth
spiced with marjoram
and memories

Allergy to Evil

my hands are itchy
scratch, scratch
go my fingers
nails raking each palm
across the dark pink life line
the deep arcs
nails against frightened flesh
phlegm-thickened throat
a rash rising in the blood

ordinary day, no
no, a closing down of breath
ten-year-old Tommy
shooting his teacher
fear for Alice
on her way to weddings

nails against flesh
a flush of fear
life so cheap
you can lose it
you can lose it
too soon
driving home
between
four thirty pm
and five

Linea Reimer Geiser

We Are Both Desperate
for a son leaving home

Feverishly you pace your basement haunt
glance at rows of childhood treasures
lined up like heroes on your bookshelf walls
leave mysteries and star-gazing
(wild attempts at reaching upper air)
wave good-bye to stelas of your past
bless and curse what made you what you are
and sends you reeling into other countries

You toss a few belongings into our old carry-all
check for ticket, for toothbrush
finger passport, pesetas, zipper shut your future
and set it gingerly beside the front door

Then your feverish hands, hands from the past
(like your grandfather's, long and slender
with your mother's nails—their round white moons)
but not comfortable, not soothing
hands we once thought would heal all they touched
but held too close to flame
your hands brush my face farewell

Leave quickly on your necessary journey
I am desperate in your presence
I cannot supply the path for your pacing
but tucked inside your tattered psyche
are twenty years of mother–love
to fend off famine when you reach the Pyrenees

64

For Tamara

A five-year-old clears a spot on a foggy train window
holds tightly to her Ukranian mother
and waves to her German father left behind
standing lonely near the tracks
while she rushes into the night
into the steely arms of Mother Russia

Silence, so long, for more than a lifetime
of frozen fingers, too little bread, dust and
shoveling coal in Siberian darkness

Fifty years of counting days and nights
never knowing the continuing family saga
on another continent
in Canada, a half-brother with her blue eyes
a half-sister the image of her younger self
an old blind father, victim of inner and outer wars
who has secretly mourned her absence
for as long as he can remember and whispers
her childhood name in his dreams

Finally political curtains rip like the temple veil
opening to summer and impossible epiphanies

But what can be said of fathers and daughters
clasped in reunion
who have missed each other's lives

Linea Reimer Geiser

Family Tree

Our years are gliding by
too soon we die

Our lives are blossoming
in golden children
stretching for the sky

Too soon they lie
beside us, leaves to dust

Their children cry

WISDOM SAYINGS

Mother-in-laws
should not arrive
swinging boxing gloves

Better to wear
smiles or clip lips together

If possible
set all family baggage
outside on the porch
and leave it there or
better yet, pack so lightly
for your visit that no one
shudders when you
ring the doorbell

Carry gifts of laughter
family stories and
a special sack of stars

Red Hot Mamma

Think
red hot
Mamma?
No!
My mum was
prim not
sassy
tender not
strident
strong
and full of
courage
full of
boundaries

Red hot
daughters?
Sometimes
when the lighting
is right
and the music
is salsa
and the moon
pulls the tides
out to sea

Easter Surprises

Last Saturday
the day before Easter
a spectacular supernova
caught the eye of astronomers
scanning with their fine-tuned instruments
the Whirlpool Galaxy for
stellar surprises
that just rolled into view

the same day
I hid six dozen bright
plastic eggs including
five with pink marshmallow chicks
a dozen with spicy jelly beans and
one with a chocolate kiss

for scampering Hannah and Nathan
Atlee and Haven
to discover
in the dead grass
between new daffodil shoots and
under the winter-weary holly
and merrily plop
into the empty straw baskets
swinging from their chubby
sweatered arms

Linea Reimer Geiser

Soup for the World

Take cabbage leaves
the big green outside leaves
take the core
white and hard
and chop, chop, chop
the housewife chop
of your mother and grandmother
Practice it

Take tomatoes
blood red, past their prime
it doesn't matter
We're making soup
We're making borscht
straight from our ancestors'
memory of steppes and fields of grain
life near the river, far off
far off in the wild Ukraine

Take the bones you boiled all day
beef or chicken clinging to them still
(use what you will—it tastes the same)
Use the broth peppered with bay leaf, allspice
onions simmering through your life
adding the flavor of peasant laughter

Do add dill
Run to the garden and pick it fresh
Pluck handfuls to drop summer scent into
winter pain

Use the big pot
cast iron hanging beside an open fire
or stuffed in prim cabinets lining
your kitchen walls

Add all the ingredients
Cook and stir and stir
with your wooden spoon
straight from Grandmother's attic
where Mother kept her few treasures
now handed down to daughters
learning to cook the old ways

Use the big pot
You must make soup for the world

baptized backwards
into light

At the Crossroads

at the crossroads
the light is blazing
I can't see where I've been
or where I'm going next

it's the rest
between cycles
sabbatical

if I stay in the light
I'm dancing in circles
maybe I'll twirl till I'm dizzy
close my eyes
and head out later

maybe all four directions
lead home

maybe the crossroads
drops down in
deeper, not
spinning out
from the center
maybe I'll sink into God
baptized backwards
into light

Linea Reimer Geiser

For Mothers and Martyrs
*for my daughter who gave birth
while I studied Anabaptist history*

Learn
Learn well
the word "travail"

Push it out between clenched teeth
give birth to it between quivering thighs

It is necessary
to deliver
the utter delight of a child
the bright surprise of the kingdom of God

Verily, Verily

The gospel
sheds our small interpretations
stands stripped
bare
bold
beautiful
with terrifying teeth

Linea Reimer Geiser

Our Cats Praise Your Name

Our cats
praise Your name

They purr, they smile
they sleep in puddles of sun
they live their catly lives
under Your benevolence

creatures who aspire
to be nothing
but Your regal lap-warmers

Washerwoman

Through the ages
her hands chapped
reddened by endless laundry
She squats near the village tap

In the midst of dust swirls, stray goats
and children pulling at her skirts
God labors
lovingly
applying strong soap
rubbing out stubborn stains
pounding out evil
against rock

Grinning with success
She prepares for festival
Her people will be clean
temporarily

Nativity

Breath of Life
Breathe in, Breathe out

Snorted puffs warm the cold cave
animal grace in beast at rest
and virgin bearing down
expelling a child
in a mighty push

Breath of Life
Breathe in, Breathe out

Suck in salvation
beast and mother and new-born babe
God flows through your lungs
Genesis rush
in a winter season

Lucifer

Lucifer and I
tumbling through space
Lucy in the sky with
diamonds
Did I ask for this descent
no
In deepest dreams evil
lurks
I have a stalker out to
get me
Lucifer, beautiful beyond stars
once beloved
falling
landing
in my soul
Will God redeem you
too
turn your midnight
madness, hyena
laughter
back to angel
song

Linea Reimer Geiser

Travel Song

September
Van Gogh sky
swirling blue and black
white light tossed in

Yes
And yellow sun and yellow moon together
Now

Aten, Sol, Diana, Luna
shining

Circle, crescent
I carry sun and moon
Pack them in my
old blue suitcase
for travels
to my older land
the Rock of Sinai

there to fling them
into new horizons

and let the darkness
shift

Cry for the World

follow the green route
high, high in the sky
circle this planet
rocking, rocking in a sea of stars

the arrows sweep clockwise
and we follow
swooping above the continents
blithely waving

through the rush of arctic air
across the poles
cryonic cold
flash freezing our bones

but on we flow
view scenes
national geographic style—
familiar daily life
high high in the sky
a god's eye tour

lose our bravado
from a distance know
seas of human blood
exploded children
famine eyes
the dead
lined up in rows
lined up in rows

Linea Reimer Geiser

even us old die-hards
the tough old birds
world leaders weep
we cry, we mourn
long before we land
we keen
o green, green planet
home

Rosemary for Remembrance

My madonnas scattered
around the house
are for remembrance
and rosemary
one of Mary's symbols

She leaves an aroma that
freshens the air
lessens spirit ills
Her herb is practical
scents something
as mundane as potatoes
is wonderful with lamb
and no surprise
she cuddles
the sweetly smiling
Lamb of God
in her arms

Linea Reimer Geiser

A Table Grace

So many poems begin at this round oak table
so much tea poured here for friends
so many prayers
rise with the steam of words
the scent of community

God, are you host when I sit alone

Are you pleased to swirl around
our shoulders when sisters and brothers
laugh and sing our lives together

Is this the table in the wilderness
holding evil outside its charm

Then should I not make this request
like the Jews of the Middle Ages
to be buried in a casket constructed
from the table of my ancestors
settled into the earth
so that I may dwell deep in the house
of the Lord forever

Flying High

Florence wants
a balloon ride
I've seen their large round shapes
tiny basket under
floating in the early
evening sky

personally
I fear the blast of heat
that makes them soar

I opt for eagle's wings
they fly higher, sweep
the silence, land
on windswept crags

but I do need
a Mother Eagle
strong feathered
watchful
who knows me feeble
in the rush
I may forget to cling

Linea Reimer Geiser

In Memory of

Jesus comes barreling
down the road in his silver pick-up
There stands Elizabeth at the corner waving
and thumbing like crazy
At ninety-nine she doesn't want to miss her ride
She's been waiting so long, seen so much
longed for home with all her might
especially since she fell and broke her bones
and thought about seeing Amos
after all these years without him

Look! The angels and Amos
piled into the back of the truck
cheering and calling "We're here! Hop in!"
No step ladder this time to climb up onto the seat
just because her legs are short
Now she floats light and feathery, ready
to cross the Jordan

That silver truck has tires that
can plow through hell and back
and pull up close to the curb
of the golden streets of heaven

Poetry Festival

I

"The lonely sea and the sky"
I recited Masefield as a teenager
never having seen the sea
and won a prize for the
nuances I gave to lonely, to sky

Lonely I knew and it carried fear
sky I knew that filled my prairie world
every day an endless dome
putting heaven and God too near
expecting at any moment to see
the Son of Man thundering
into view on a flaming silver steed
slashing his sword between good and evil
and how could I be sure that
I had make the cut or would be cast
lonely into hell

The sky gave no clue
to my future

II

Many seas later
I can finish the poem I started
to intone in tenth grade—"the lonely sea"
but my mood has changed
the sea, waves endlessly washing
the swish of crest unrolling on shore

I am not like the ancient Hebrews
terrified that Tiamat will devour me
only in deepest dreams do tsunamis overwhelm

I catch an endless certainty
watching, knowing the next
swell will roll in and break and retreat

Maybe I remember our first home before
we washed ashore in Eden
Now that I am a land creature
my blood still retains the ocean salt
the rhythm that is more than lonely
that rocks me to eternity

III

Maybe this poem is a chameleon
I'm afraid of the sea sometimes
while sky, sky is a changing
glory over my head
and lonely comes and goes

At Prayer
for Gertrude

Quiet
in a spinning space
singing out past webbed despair

Cries
arc the dark
like shooting stars
like jewels
cut on the lathe of pain
polished with meticulous care

Woman
wraps in her shawl of prayer

Linea Reimer Geiser

One Easter in the Sweet Spring Rain

One day half-way between birth and old age
we danced on the dead of Violett Cemetery

One Easter in the sweet spring rain we sang
our hallelujah promises to ourselves
and to the waiting ones beneath

We raised our arms, clasped hands
and spun in merry circles between bright daffodils
our feet in motion, thumping signals with each beat
that for the present we shared space but not time
and for the future we trusted them to share eternity

One Easter in the sweet spring rain we sang

"Unter Deinem Sanften Fittich"
(Under Your Soft Feathers)

When I won't can't don't stop
long enough for a loving,
Grandmother God
swoops me up in her arms
for a hug
a cheek to cheek and reminder
that I am her treasure

We look at sky shadowed
by flocks gathering
for fall migration

She tells me stories
about birds on the wing
their marvelous feathers
lifting them across oceans

She tells me
her arms are like feathers
light to the touch, strong to warm
sure to protect
a comfort for the coldest
longest journey home

Linea Reimer Geiser

On the Green Grass

Our laughter
peals through late after-glow

In the yard of the undertaker
we lose ourselves
in one more game

Whose turn will it be?

The Gatekeeper
stalks us methodically
crunching softly on loose gravel
peering behind every looming bush
snatching at shadows

while we, tweaking his nose
race gleefully by
to the charmed circle of safety
and Our Father's
"Home free!"

Linea Reimer Geiser

About the Poet

Linea Reimer Geiser was born in Winnipeg, Manitoba, and raised in the Russian Mennonite community of Steinbach, Manitoba. A wife, mother, and grandmother, she now lives in Goshen, Indiana, with her husband and two pet cats. Her undergraduate degree is from Goshen (Indiana) College and her Master of Divinity degree from Associate Mennonite Biblical Seminary at Elkhart, Indiana. She has had poems published in periodicals such as *The Mennonite, Gospel Herald, Purpose, Heritage Country, Christian Living, WMSC Voice, Church Teachers*, as well as in *Born Giving Birth* and *Hymnal: a Worship Book*. This is her first book of poetry.

Printed in the United States
867800004B